Property of
Gibsons Elementary Library

SCIENCE ISSUES

Global warming

Pennie Stoyles, Peter Pentland, and David Demant

A+

This edition first published in 2004 in the United States of America by
Smart Apple Media.

Smart Apple Media
1980 Lookout Drive
North Mankato
Minnesota 56003

Library of Congress Cataloging-in-Publication Data

Stoyles, Pennie.
Global warming / by Pennie Stoyles, Peter Pentland, and David Demant.
p. cm. — (Science issues)

Includes index.
Summary: Discusses two sides of issues related to global warming—whether the climate change will have good or bad effects, whether or not greenhouse gases should be reduced, and whether forests should be cleared for farms.

ISBN 1-58340-328-0
1. Global warming—Juvenile literature. [1. Global warming.] I. Pentland, Peter. II. Demant, David. III. Title.
QC981.8.G56S83 2003
363.738'4—dc21 2002044633

First Edition
9 8 7 6 5 4 3 2 1

First published in 2003 by
MACMILLAN EDUCATION AUSTRALIA PTY LTD
627 Chapel Street, South Yarra, Australia 3141

Associated companies and representatives throughout the world.

Edited by Sally Woollett
Text and cover design by Polar Design Pty Ltd
Illustrations by Alan Laver, Shelly Communications
Photo research by Jes Senbergs

Printed in Thailand

Acknowledgements
The author and the publisher are grateful to the following for permission to reproduce copyright material:

Cover photograph: gas flaring at an oil well, courtesy of Y. Gladu—Explorer/Auscape.

AAP Image, p. 11; Australian Picture Library/Corbis, pp. 21, 25; BHP Coal, p. 26; Coo-ee Picture Library, pp. 5, 17, 18; The DW Stock Picture Library, p. 29; Getty Images, pp. 12, 14, 15, 23, 28; Bob Girdo, www.girdo.com, p. 4; Y. Gladu—Explorer/Auscape, p. 19; Dale Mann/Retrospect, p. 16; NASA, p. 6; Photolibrary.com, pp. 22, 27; Reuters, pp. 9, 30.

Graph on p. 13 based on data sourced from http://cdiac.esd.ornl.gov/ftp/trends/temp/vostok/vostok.1999.temp.dat, with thanks to the researchers at Laboratoire de Glaciologie et de Geophysique de l'Environnement and Laboratoire des Sciences du Climat et de l'Environment, France, Arctic and Antarctic Research Institute, St. Petersburg, and Institute of Geography, Moscow.

Contents

Glossary words
When a word is printed in **bold** you can look up its meaning in the Glossary on page 31.

Look out for these questions.
Try to think about them while you read each issue in this book.

Global warming

Tuvalu is a group of nine coral islands in the South Pacific Ocean. The islands have a total area of about 10 square miles (26 sq km). They have a population of around 11,000 people. The highest point in Tuvalu is 16.4 feet (5 m) above sea level.

The main economic activities of Tuvalu are **subsistence farming** and fishing. There are no streams or rivers. To get water, the Tuvalese people catch and store rainwater and purify seawater.

Global warming is the result of an increase in the average temperature of Earth's surface and **atmosphere**. If the atmosphere heats up, some of the ice on Earth could melt and flow into the oceans. This will make the level of the sea rise. If this happens, much of Tuvalu is at risk of being covered by sea.

Another concern is that global warming may cause more storms and that these storms may cause more damage.

Tuvalu is not the only place in the world that would be affected in this way by global warming. Global warming is predicted to have many other effects on Earth.

Scientists such as meteorologists work to find out more about global warming. They:

- look for evidence of global warming
- study weather patterns and climates
- find out how gases such as **carbon dioxide** affect global warming.

Funafuti lagoon in Tuvalu.

Global warming is a science issue

What will happen to the people of Tuvalu if the sea level rises? Where will they live?

Scientific evidence suggests that global warming is happening, but scientists have different opinions about what is causing it. There are also people who have not yet made up their minds. This makes global warming a science issue.

Different points of view

Sometimes you have to decide what you think about something. Before you decide whether something is good or bad, or right or wrong, you usually try to find out about the subject and listen to what other people think. There may be two opposite points of view. Different people or groups may have several different views. This is what makes something an issue.

Can you trust everything you read and hear? It is a good idea to look carefully at the people who are arguing about an issue. Do they know all of the facts? Are they only giving one side of the issue because they have something to gain? You should not simply accept what people say. Think about what they say and why they say it.

Think about the source of your information before you accept it.

THIS BOOK will help you understand more about some global warming issues. It tries to be balanced. Two sides of each issue are presented to help you to decide what *you* think.

You will:

- find out about **climate** change
- find out about **greenhouse gases**
- discover the relationship between forests and the atmosphere
- learn how to produce less greenhouse gas.

Understanding global warming

The atmosphere

Earth's atmosphere is a layer of gases surrounding the planet. The layer is very thin (about 370 miles or 600 km) compared to the thickness of Earth, which is just under 8,078 miles (13,000 km). The atmosphere stays around the planet because gravity holds it down.

Layers of the atmosphere

The atmosphere can be divided into four layers. The layer next to Earth is called the troposphere. The troposphere is about 9 miles (15 km) high and is where most of our weather happens. The temperature drops as you go higher.

The next layer is the stratosphere. Pilots prefer to fly in this layer because there is not much bad weather. In the stratosphere, the temperature rises as you go higher. This is because it contains a gas called ozone, which reacts with sunlight to cause heating. The upper two layers of the atmosphere are called the mesosphere and the thermosphere.

^ The atmosphere is very thin compared to the size of Earth. The moon does not have enough gravity to hold down an atmosphere.

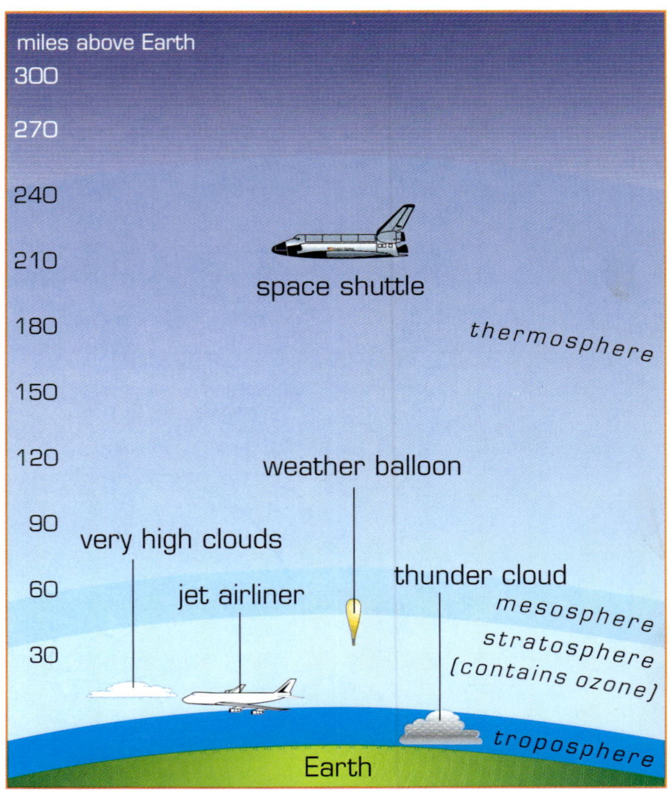

>> The atmosphere is made of four layers.

Hot spot

Earth's atmosphere consists of 78 percent nitrogen, 21 percent oxygen, and 1 percent of other gases.

The greenhouse effect

A greenhouse is a glass building used for growing plants in cold weather. Visible light from the Sun passes through the glass. It is **absorbed** by the plants and the inside of the building. Some of the light energy is changed into heat, most of which is trapped inside the greenhouse by the glass. Some heat escapes out of the glass. The trapped heat raises the temperature inside the greenhouse.

Earth's atmosphere behaves like the glass in a greenhouse. Visible light and some **ultraviolet light** from the Sun pass through the atmosphere. Some light "bounces" off the clouds and the surface of Earth back into space. Plants use some of the light to grow. The rest of the light is changed into heat energy.

Some heat energy is sent back towards space. The rest of the heat energy remains and makes the surface of Earth hotter. The atmosphere absorbs some of the heat and it gets hotter. This is called the **greenhouse effect**.

The atmosphere contains certain gases which help to keep the heat in. These are called greenhouse gases. They make up less than 1 percent of the atmosphere. The main gases that cause the greenhouse effect are carbon dioxide, water vapor, ozone, and methane. Although there are very small amounts of them in the atmosphere, they are very important.

Hot spot

The average temperature of Earth is much greater than it would be if the greenhouse gases were not present in the atmosphere.

Some heat energy from the Sun "bounces" back into space and some is trapped in Earth's atmosphere.

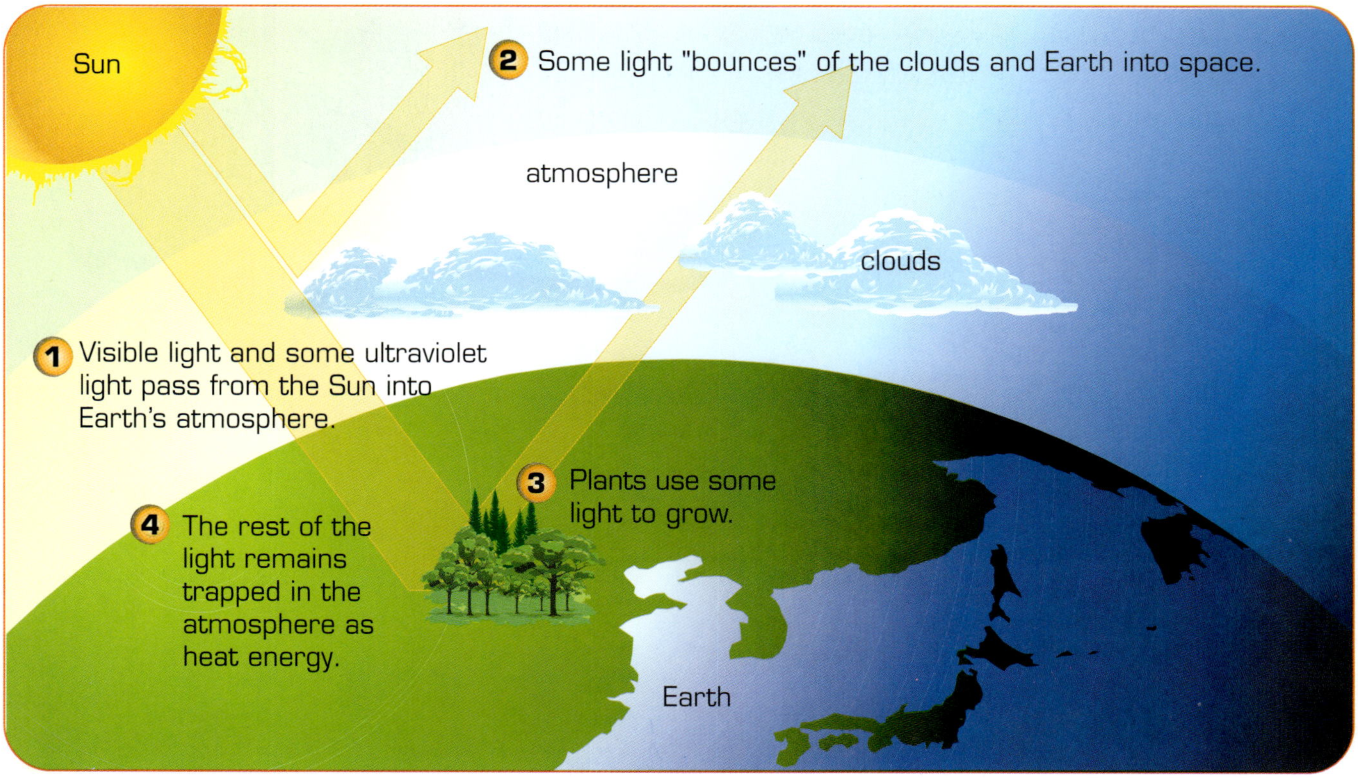

Carbon dioxide

Carbon dioxide is a greenhouse gas. It contains carbon, which is found in all living things. In nature, carbon is continually changed into carbon dioxide and back again into carbon. Carbon passes from living things into the environment and then back again into other living things. This is called the **carbon cycle**.

Living things take in carbon from their environment. People take in carbon when they eat food, because carbon is a part of the plant and animal products that make our food. When plants and animals die they rot and return carbon to the soil.

During the day, plants take in carbon dioxide through their leaves to make food by a process called **photosynthesis**. Plants release carbon dioxide at night when there is not enough light to drive the process of photosynthesis. Animals release carbon dioxide when they breathe out.

Fossil fuels such as coal, oil, gasoline, and natural gas contain carbon. These fuels come mainly from the remains of plants that lived millions of years ago. They removed carbon dioxide from the air when they were alive. The fuels will release it back into the air when they are burned.

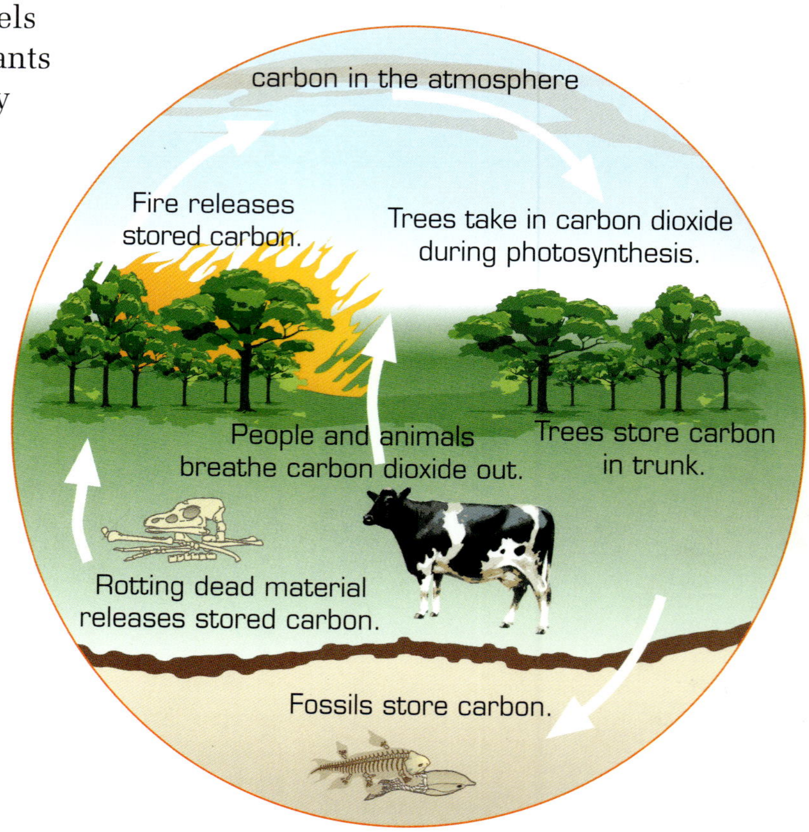

Carbon is cycled between living things in the environment.

Hot spot

Carbon atoms in your body could have once been in the body of a dinosaur!

Effects of global warming

Greenhouse gases such as carbon dioxide warm the planet by a process called global warming. Global warming could cause:

- a rise in the sea level
- climate changes in regions around the world.

Rise in sea levels

A lot of water is stored in Earth's polar ice caps, in glaciers and permanent snow caps on mountains, and as frozen ground in the Arctic regions. If the world gets warmer, some of this ice will melt and flow into the oceans, causing the sea level to rise.

As the water in the oceans gets warmer it will take up more space. This will also cause the sea level to rise.

Climate change

An increase in the average temperature of the atmosphere will change the weather patterns and climates of regions around the world. An average increase means the temperature would increase overall, but not necessarily everywhere. Some regions may become hotter and other regions cooler.

Climate change could cause more storms, and the storms could be more destructive. Climate change could turn some regions into deserts as the rainfall lessens. It could cause storms that flood farmlands.

Global warming could result in violent storms that flood the land.

ISSUE 1

Climate change

Climate reports from around the world

United Kingdom
A study of six species of birds found that they were nesting and laying their eggs about nine days earlier in the year than 25 years previously.

Europe
Plants and animals are moving into regions closer to the poles of Earth because these regions are becoming warmer. For example, 22 out of 35 species of butterflies studied have moved further north by 25 to 155 miles (40–250 km).

Russia
Glaciers around the world are shrinking. In the Russian Caucasus Mountains, half the volume of the ice in glaciers disappeared during the twentieth century.

Alaska
Four out of the five earliest river thaws on record occurred since 1990.

Kenya
Over 90 percent of the Lewis Glacier disappeared during the twentieth century.

Antarctica
The Adélie penguin population has been reduced by one-third between 1975 and 2000. The area of winter ice available to them has been reduced.

Australia and Mexico
Coral reef damage has been reported all over the world including the Great Barrier Reef in Australia, and in Mexico.

United States
Trees are flowering earlier in the year. Cherry trees in Washington, D.C., are now reaching the peak of their flowering period many days earlier than they did 80 years ago.

Is the climate changing?

Reports from around the world seem to suggest that some parts of Earth are getting warmer. Many of these reports were collected by the Intergovernmental Panel on Climate Change (IPCC) in 2001. Do these reports mean that all of Earth is getting warmer? Is this unusual and should we be worried about it?

What are the issues about climate change?

If climate change is happening, it may be because of human activities. It may be because Earth is going through a normal cycle of change. Whatever the reason, climate change may affect many people in the future.

It is difficult for scientists to predict the effects of climate change on particular regions of the world. This is because the climate of a region is the average of all the local weather conditions over many years. It is very difficult to predict the weather in a local area.

- Q What causes climate change?
- Q How is climate change measured?
- Q How do people cause climate change?
- Q How will climate change affect the environment?

Glacier measurements have shown that most glaciers are shrinking.

Recording climate change

One way to find out if the climate is changing is to look at weather records from the past. People only started keeping weather records in the 1860s. So how do we know what happened hundreds of thousands of years ago? Scientists use rocks, trees, and ice from glaciers and ice caps to find out about the past.

Rocks

Rocks give us information about temperature and rainfall for millions of years into the past. Fossils taken from layers that were once at the bottom of seas can be used to show how the temperature varied over millions of years.

Trees

Many trees can grow for over 1,000 years. A tree adds layers called tree rings to the outside of its trunk as it grows. Tree rings can show what the seasons were like when the tree was growing. When the climate is warmer, the rings are thicker, because the tree grows faster in warmer weather.

Ice

Information can be obtained by drilling into the ice in places such as Greenland and Antarctica. The ice is removed as a long tube, called a core. The top of the core contains ice that came from snow that fell in this century. The ice gets older towards the bottom of the core. The ice contains trapped air, which scientists can analyze. They are able to tell what Earth's climate was like from the oxygen content of the air.

>> This is the end view of a tree that has been cut down. You can see that some rings are thicker than others.

Natural climate change

Changes in climate can be caused by natural events. These natural events could warm or cool Earth.

Scientists believe that Earth has gone through several **ice ages** in the last 400,000 years. Each ice age lasted about 100,000 years. In between ice ages Earth warmed up again for about 15,000 years.

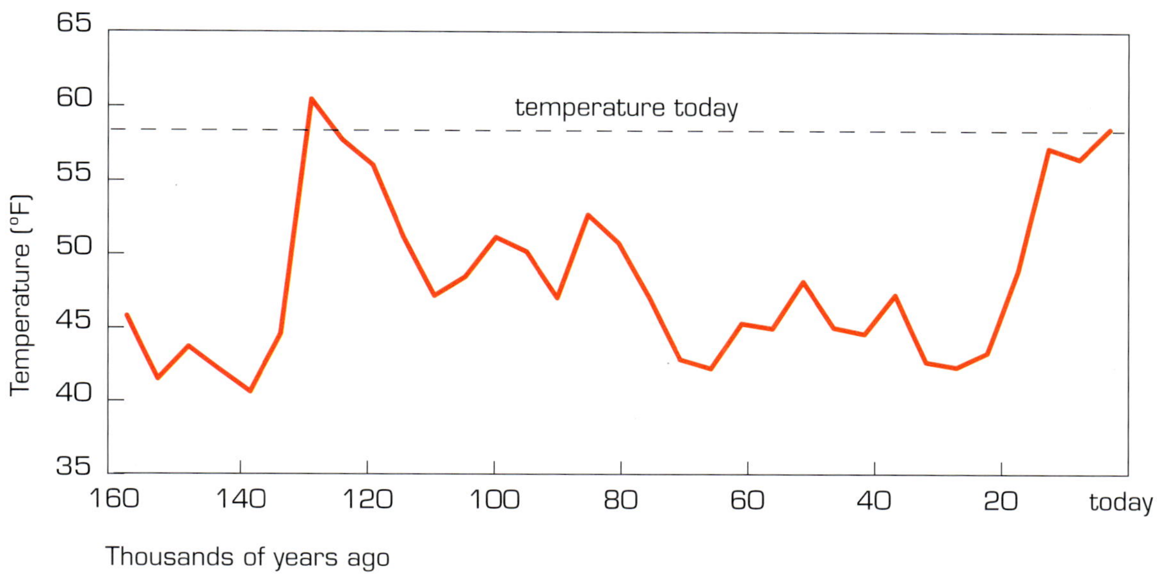

^ This graph shows that Earth's climate has warmed and cooled many times. We can also see that we are now in a warm period that has followed a very long cool period. This cool period started with a big drop in temperature (about 16 degrees Fahrenheit) about 130,000 years ago.

Scientists think that the ice ages are caused by a combination of natural events. Earth moved further from the Sun and changed its tilt.

Earth's temperature began to get warmer about 18,000 years ago. Since then, the average temperature of Earth's atmosphere has risen by about 9 degrees Fahrenheit. The ice sheets that covered much of the world melted, causing the level of the oceans to rise by 394 feet (120 m).

If a meteor hit Earth, or a huge volcano erupted, the atmosphere would be filled with huge clouds of dust. The dust would block out the Sun and cause the temperature to fall.

Climate change and people

Over the past 200 years, human activities have increased the amounts of greenhouse gases in Earth's atmosphere. Driving cars, using electricity, running factories, and other activities make greenhouse gases. In this time, the amount of carbon dioxide has increased by about 30 percent. Many people believe that these extra greenhouse gases will cause global warming, which will change the climates of different parts of the world.

^ In what ways do the activities in this city contribute to climate change?

Global warming will not lead to an even increase in temperature across the surface of the world. It will affect different places in different ways. Whether a place has milder winters and longer growing seasons or hotter, more extreme summers and less rainfall depends on where it is and the changes to its weather patterns. The changes may have good or bad effects on activities such as farming and forestry.

Some places may actually become cooler if they get more winds that come from across the oceans or from Earth's colder polar regions. Other places may become hotter and drier if they get more winds that come from across deserts or from Earth's hotter equatorial regions.

Global warming might even trigger a sudden onset of a new ice age. This may happen if a warm ocean current called the North Atlantic Gulf Stream is stopped. This could be caused by melting glaciers and floods in northern Europe.

v This diagram shows some of the natural and human factors that affect our planet's climate.

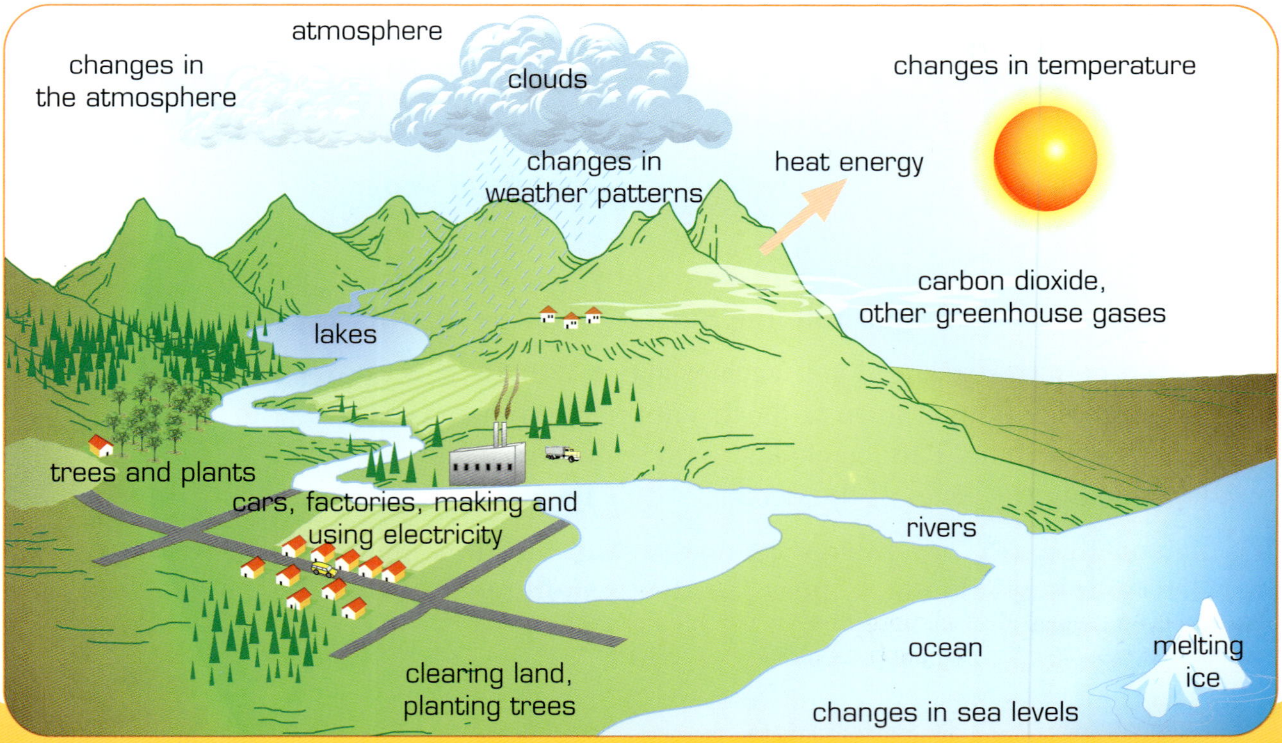

DEBATE

The climate change debate

The average temperature of Earth is increasing. This could be due to a natural cycle Earth is going through or because of human activities or both. Some people are very worried that climate change will have bad effects, others think that there may be good effects.

Arguments for

Some people believe that the effects of climate change will be good because:

- ✓ some dry regions might get an increased water supply
- ✓ as the weather in the regions near the poles becomes less cold, there will be a decreased number of deaths as a result of exposure to extreme conditions
- ✓ the winters will be milder and there will be less demand for energy for heating.

Arguments against

Other people believe that the effects of climate change will be bad because:

- ✗ sea levels will rise. This will cause millions of people to leave their lands and become refugees
- ✗ there will be less land for farming as dry regions get hotter and drier
- ✗ there will be more destructive storms such as tropical cyclones, hurricanes, and tornadoes
- ✗ there will be an increase in energy use due to the use of air conditioners in hot weather periods.

What is your opinion?

Q Are changes in weather part of a natural cycle?

Q Are human activities changing the weather?

Q Should we be worried about climate change?

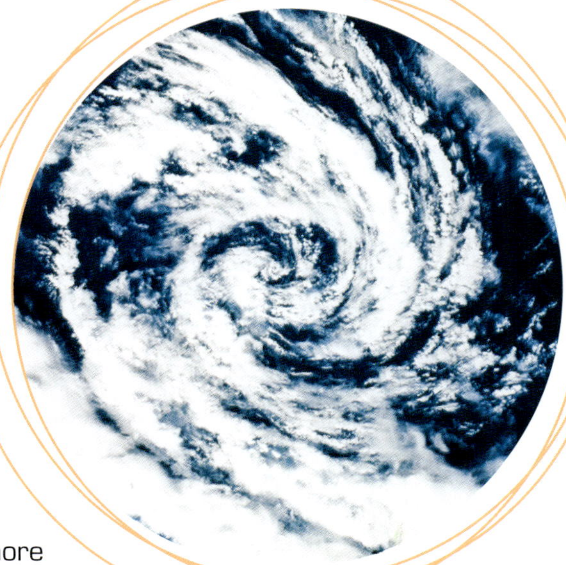

>> Some people believe that climate change will cause more destructive weather events such as tropical cyclones.

ISSUE 2

Greenhouse gases

Living in a greenhouse home

A typical house in a place such as northern America makes greenhouse gases every day. The Green family lives in just such a house. Here is how the Greens make greenhouse gases.

Cooking and heating with gas

Most members of the Green household have a shower in the morning. Their hot water system uses natural gas. They cook most of their meals on gas hot plates, which also use natural gas. Every time they turn on the oven or a hot water faucet they are burning natural gas, which produces greenhouse gases.

Transportation

The adult Greens take turns driving their children to school. Every gallon of fuel used by a car produces about 21 pounds of greenhouse gases (1 l produces 2.5 kg).

Using electricity

After work and school the Greens sometimes like to watch television or listen to music on their sound system. In the winter they often heat their living room with a space heater and in the summer they use an air conditioner. Mr. Green is always reminding his daughter to turn the light off in her room when she is not using it.

The Greens' electricity is made by burning fossil fuel in a power station. Every time they use electricity they are sending greenhouse gases into the air.

Hot spot

Operating a 60-watt lightbulb for 15 hours produces about 2.2 pounds (1 kg) of greenhouse gases back at the power station.

^ How much greenhouse gas do you make at home?

How humans make greenhouse gases

Imagine life without cars, plastic wrap, paperboard boxes, televisions, toilet paper, radio stations, hamburgers, electricity, public transportation, breakfast cereal, and telephones. Greenhouse gases are produced when all of these things (and many more) are made or used.

Greenhouse gases are naturally occurring, but human activities today produce more of them than in the past.

>> This electricity power station burns coal from the nearby open cut mine. This process makes greenhouse gases.

What are the issues about greenhouse gases?

Are the greenhouse gases produced by humans causing global warming? If so, is this a good or a bad thing?

Greenhouse gases affect all countries in the world, no matter where they are made. Should the countries that make a lot of greenhouse gases change the way they make and use energy?

Q How are greenhouse gases made?

Q Which countries make the most greenhouse gases?

Q Should governments be doing more to control greenhouse gases?

Q What choices would you make to reduce greenhouse gases?

The enhanced greenhouse effect

When greenhouse gases are added to the atmosphere by the activities of people, the atmosphere gets warmer. This is called the **enhanced greenhouse effect**.

The main gases that cause the enhanced greenhouse effect are carbon dioxide, methane, chlorofluorocarbons (CFCs), ozone, and nitrous oxides.

Carbon dioxide

Carbon dioxide is a colorless, odorless gas that is heavier than air. It is produced when plant or animal matter is burned.

Methane

Methane is a colorless, odorless gas that is lighter than air. It traps 30 times more heat than the same amount of carbon dioxide. The amount of methane in the atmosphere has doubled over the past 100 years.

CFCs, nitrous oxide, and ozone

CFCs are gases that are made by industrial processes.

Nitrous oxide is produced by fossil fuel power stations and motor vehicles.

Ozone protects us from ultraviolet light from the Sun. It is very good at trapping heat.

These three gases are responsible for a very small part of the enhanced greenhouse effect.

The gas from the oxen's stomachs and from the plant matter in this field is methane gas.

Activities that make greenhouse gases

People make greenhouse gases when they burn fuels for power, cooking, and heating. Greenhouse gases are also made during building and farming.

Burning fuels

When fossil fuels are burned they produce greenhouse gases.

Fossil fuels are burned:

- to make electricity
- to power cars, trucks, airplanes, and ships
- for heating and cooking.

When oil is pumped from the ground, sometimes natural gas is released. This is burned to reduce pressure in the well or to get rid of small amounts that are not useful.

When you burn wood in a fire or a grill you make greenhouse gases. Forest fires also release greenhouse gases.

Cement

Greenhouse gases are released when cement and lime are made. Cement is used in the building industry to make house foundations.

Waste and farming

Greenhouse gases are released when waste materials are burned in city dumps. Methane gas is made by garbage dumps as the garbage rots.

Farms supply a lot of the world's food. Cows, buffalo, sheep, and goats make a lot of methane gas in their digestive systems. Rice farming and rotting manure also produce methane.

Refrigerators and aerosols

Greenhouse gases such as CFCs and methane were used in air conditioners and refrigerators. They were also used in aerosols. Newer products are no longer made with these gases.

<<
Flaring is the burning of natural gas at an oil well.

Who makes the most greenhouse gas?

Different countries produce different amounts of greenhouse gas. Developed countries use more energy than less developed ones. Carbon dioxide is the most significant greenhouse gas, so it is useful to compare the amounts of carbon dioxide that different countries produce.

Hot spot

The U.S. has only 5 percent of the world's population yet it is responsible for about 22 percent of the world's carbon dioxide production from human activities.

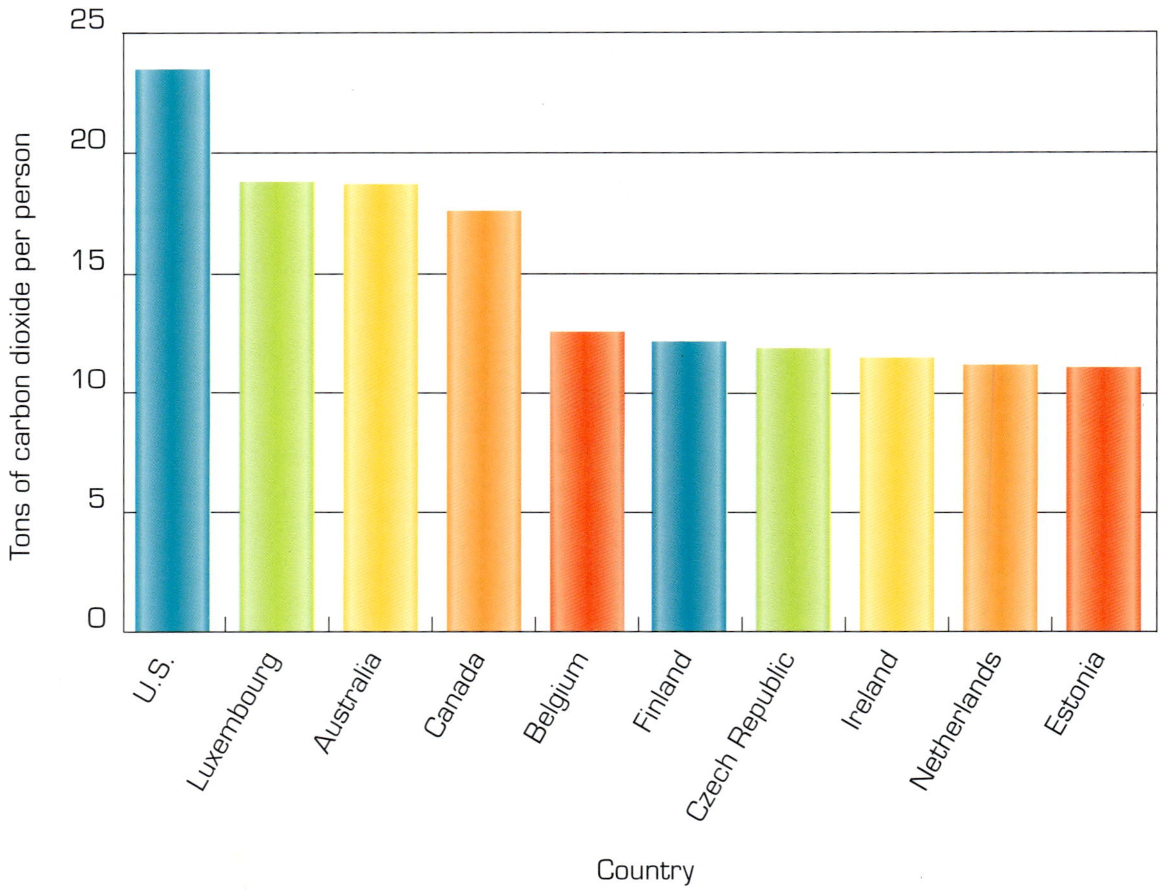

This graph shows the ten highest producers of carbon dioxide gas per person in 1999.

The figures shown in the graph take into account the populations of the countries. Working out the carbon dioxide produced per person takes into account the carbon dioxide produced by the industries of the countries, not just the amount that each person is responsible for.

What are governments doing about greenhouse gas?

Too much greenhouse gas in the atmosphere is a worldwide problem. Countries of the world have been meeting to try to work out what to do about it.

The Kyoto Protocol

In 1997, the **United Nations** met in Kyoto, Japan to discuss climate change. The member countries produced the **Kyoto Protocol**, which is a set of rules that countries can follow to help reduce greenhouse gases and stop the planet from heating up.

Here are some of the rules of the Kyoto Protocol:

- Developed countries should reduce their total production of six greenhouse gases by at least 5 percent of 1990 levels by 2012.
- The countries should become more efficient in using energy.
- Places that store or use up greenhouse gases should be protected or made bigger. This refers to places like forests and oceans.
- Farms that do not rely on using a lot of energy or chemicals should be encouraged.
- Countries should try to get their energy from **renewable sources**. (Fossil fuels such as coal, oil, and gas are not renewable.)
- Industries that make a lot of greenhouse gases should be encouraged to become more efficient.
- Methane gas should be collected from waste disposal places.

Not all countries are following the rules. Sometimes this is because it is easier to keep doing things the way they have always been doing them. It is easier not to change.

>>
This meeting of the United Nations was about the Kyoto Protocol. The meeting happened in Morocco in 2001.

Making less greenhouse gas

Greenhouse gases are made when you use energy. People who want to reduce greenhouse gases think that we should save energy or use energy sources that do not make greenhouse gases.

Saving energy

- Choose electrical appliances that use less energy.
- Turn off lights and appliances when you are not using them.
- Use cold water to wash clothes.
- Use a solar hot water system.
- Insulate your house so you do not have to use heating and cooling appliances.
- Design houses that let in winter sunlight for heating, and stay cool by keeping out summer sunlight.
- Use public transportation, or ride a bike or walk when traveling short distances.

>>
This room allows the winter sunlight in to keep the room warm without a heater.

Sources that do not make greenhouse gases

Some energy sources do not run out. These energy sources are called renewable or sustainable sources.

- Solar energy comes from the Sun. It is used to heat water and buildings or it can be changed into electricity using solar cells. Solar cells are expensive to produce.
- Wind energy is caused by the Sun as it heats Earth's surface. It can be changed into electricity. Wind farms are noisy and, some people say, ugly. They are only useful in places where there is a reliable supply of wind.
- Hydro-electricity uses the energy of falling water. This can be done by building dams across rivers. This floods forests and land. There are not many places where hydro-electricity can be produced.

DEBATE

The greenhouse gases debate

Greenhouse gases are produced when we make energy for homes, transportation, and industry. As the world's population increases in the future there will be a greater need for energy and food. More greenhouse gases will be made.

Arguments for

Some people believe that we need to make more greenhouse gases or make them at the same rate because:

- the world needs energy for transportation. Burning gasoline is a cheap way of providing this energy.
- the world needs electricity for homes, transportation, entertainment, and industry. Burning fossil fuels is a cheap way of making electricity.
- the world's growing population will need more food and energy. Meeting this need means that more fossil fuels will have to be burned and that more greenhouse gases will have to be produced.

Arguments against

Other people feel that we should reduce the amounts of greenhouse gases we produce because:

- the world has to reduce the effects of global warming and climate change
- there are alternative ways of producing energy that do not make as much greenhouse gas
- making more energy is not necessary. People can save energy by being more efficient with their energy use.

These solar cells use sunlight to make energy without making greenhouse gases.

What is your opinion?

Q Do you agree with the rules of the Kyoto Protocol?

Q Should people be more efficient in their use of energy?

Q Should we develop renewable ways of making energy?

ISSUE 3

Forests or farms?

Amazon rain forest

The Amazon rain forest in the Amazon Basin is the largest and most dense rain forest in the world. It had an original area of more than 1,930,500 square miles (5,000,000 sq km).

Many people live on the edge of the Amazon rain forest. They survive by farming, growing vegetables and fruit. They might also have chickens and a few animals for eggs and meat. This is called subsistence farming.

The land on the edge of the Amazon is constantly being cleared to make room for cattle, pastures, and food crops. This forces the subsistence farmers from their land. The cleared land loses its **nutrients** in a few years so more forest has to be cleared.

The Amazon rain forest is also logged. This provides timber for buildings and furniture and woodchips for making particle board and paper. Loggers in the rain forest remove mature trees.

People who have been forced from their farms at the edge of the forest follow the roads built by the loggers into the forest. They burn and clear the places where the big trees were removed so they can plant crops. People like these are said to be responsible for 60 percent of the loss of the world's tropical rain forests.

<< The Amazon rain forest is the world's biggest rain forest.

Forests and carbon dioxide

Carbon is essential for life on Earth. The carbon cycle explains the way that carbon is used and reused by living things. Large areas of big plants like forest trees are called **carbon sinks** because they remove carbon from the atmosphere.

Carbon dioxide is the main greenhouse gas. Plants take in carbon dioxide and release oxygen as a part of a process called photosynthesis.

>>
Logging roads like this one into the Amazon rain forest allow large machinery in to log the forest faster.

What are the issues about forests or farms?

Forests help to slow down global warming by removing carbon dioxide from the air. They also contain many different plants and animals. Rain forests are being cut down to make farms to produce more food to feed more people. The wood is needed to build houses and furniture. People have different opinions about keeping the forests or clearing them to grow food.

Hot spot

The Rainforest Action Network estimates that rain forests around the world are being cleared at a rate of 2.47 acres (about 1 h) every second.

Q Why are forests important?

Q How good are forests at removing greenhouse gases?

Q Should forests be cut down to make way for farms or dams?

Carbon sinks

A carbon sink is a place where carbon is stored. Earth has three main carbon sinks.

Forests

Forests are carbon sinks because the trees and other plants have soaked up carbon dioxide and they store it inside themselves. The more trees and other plants that there are in the forest, the more carbon is stored, and the more carbon dioxide is removed from the atmosphere.

Plants grow bigger if there is more carbon dioxide in the air. Scientists believe that trees are growing bigger. The bigger trees soak up more carbon dioxide!

Fossil fuels

All the coal, oil, and natural gas in the ground are a store of carbon. Millions of years ago fossil fuels were living things. So fossil fuels contain carbon that came from carbon dioxide that was removed from the air millions of years ago. When we burn fossil fuels, we release carbon dioxide back into the air.

Oceans

Carbon dioxide **dissolves** in water. The oceans contain millions of tons of dissolved carbon dioxide. If the oceans become warmer, then they will not be able to store as much carbon dioxide.

<<
This is a wall of an open cut coal mine. It is made of coal, which is a fossil fuel.

The importance of forests

Forests such as rain forests act as carbon sinks in the carbon cycle. The trees in rain forests usually have large wide leaves for catching sunlight and soaking up the greenhouse gas carbon dioxide.

Hot spot

Rain forests are thought to contain many undiscovered species of plants that might be used to make medicines.

There are many kinds of forest. Tropical rain forests are found near the **equator** in South America, Asia, and Africa. Temperate rain forests are found in cooler regions away from the tropics.

A rain forest has lots of big trees and the rainfall in a year is high (more than 98 inches or 250 cm). The forests grow because of the high rainfalls. When the trees are cleared for timber and farms, nutrients are quickly washed from the soil. This means that the land quickly becomes useless for farming.

Why are forests logged?

People plant forests to use for buildings, furniture, and paper. These are called plantation forests. Plantation forests have fast-growing trees such as pines. These can be harvested 20 to 50 years after the trees have been planted. Plantation forests do not contain the variety of different plants and animals that are found in naturally occurring forests.

Other types of trees are not grown in plantations. They are taken from wilderness and old-growth forests. Once they are cut down, they take hundreds of years to grow back.

>>
This is a satellite picture of the Amazon rain forest. It had an original area of about 1,930,500 square miles (5,000,000 km). It is estimated that over 13 percent of this area has been destroyed.

The importance of farms

The world's human population

The United Nations estimates that the world's population will increase from six billion in the year 1999 to just over nine billion by the year 2050. That means that there will be three billion more people needing food and building materials.

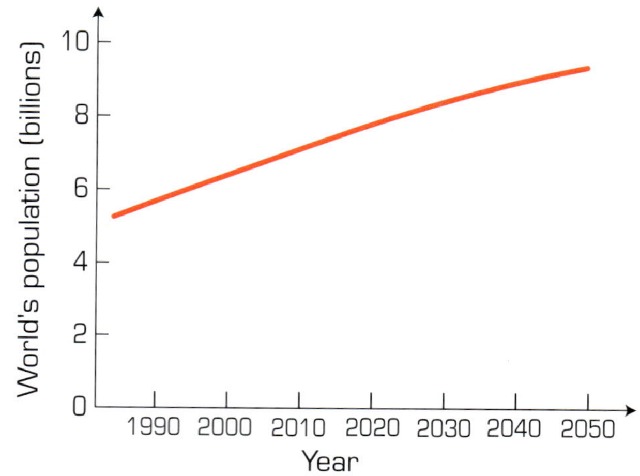

^ The world's population is growing quickly.

Food

Most of our food is grown on farms or caught in the oceans. Providing enough food for the world's increasing population could be done by:

- clearing forests to increase the amount of land used for farming
- developing better farming techniques
- better managing water resources for growing crops
- developing crops and animals to give more food from the farms we already have.

Crops are carbon sinks

Crops also remove carbon dioxide from the atmosphere. Some crops such as corn are very leafy. American corn crops are believed to be removing a lot more carbon dioxide than scientists had originally thought they would.

Plants grow better when there is more carbon dioxide in the air. They grow bigger and remove some of the extra carbon dioxide. Scientists think this effect is slowing the rate of global warming.

<<
Forests are cleared to provide land for farms and food for an increasing world population.

DEBATE

The forests or farms debate

Clearing forests provides wood for housing and furniture. It also provides farmland to grow food. However, forests remove one of the greenhouse gases, carbon dioxide, from the air. Should we preserve forests?

Arguments for

Some people believe that forests are the lungs of the world and that we should stop clearing forests because:

- ✓ forests are needed as carbon sinks
- ✓ plantation forests are able to provide enough wood for housing and furniture
- ✓ we should be recycling paper and building materials instead.

Arguments against

Other people believe that clearing forests is acceptable because:

- ✗ the population of the world is getting bigger. The world needs more land to grow food to feed them.
- ✗ plants grow better when there is more carbon dioxide in the air
- ✗ forests are only partly responsible for removing carbon dioxide from the atmosphere
- ✗ scientists are still trying to identify how carbon dioxide is being removed from the air.

What is your opinion?

Q Should forests be cleared for farms?

Q Do grasslands and crops remove as much carbon dioxide as the forests they replace?

<<
Should we stop clearing forests for farms?

Summary

The world's population is growing quickly. Over the past 200 years, humans have added a lot of greenhouse gases to the atmosphere. Rain forests are being cleared for timber and farms. In this book, some of the issues that surround global warming have been raised.

ISSUE 1 Climate change

- The world's climate is changing.
- Climate change could be due to natural cycles or human activities.
- A changing climate could lead to a rise in sea levels, floods in some areas, and drought conditions in others.

Q What will happen to people living in areas affected by climate change?

ISSUE 2 Greenhouse gases

- Using energy usually makes greenhouses gases.
- Many of the wealthiest countries make the most greenhouse gases.
- The Kyoto Protocol is a set of rules about producing less greenhouse gases.

Q Should we try to save energy to make less greenhouse gas?

ISSUE 3 Forests or farms?

- Farms are needed to grow food for the increasing world population.
- Forests remove carbon dioxide from the air.
- Forests are not the only way that carbon dioxide is removed.

Q Is there a way to keep the forests and feed the population?

THE FUTURE

One way to reduce global warming is to reduce greenhouse gases. An Australian inventor, Mr. John Harrison, has invented an eco-cement. He claims that one ton of this cement will absorb 0.36 tons of carbon dioxide from the atmosphere as it hardens (1 t absorbs 0.4 t). The cement would turn buildings into carbon sinks.

Glossary

absorbed	taken up by one substance into another; for example, a towel absorbs water from your hands
atmosphere	a layer of gases surrounding Earth. It is held there by Earth's gravity.
carbon cycle	a natural process in which carbon is used and recycled
carbon dioxide	a colorless, odorless gas that helps trap heat in the atmosphere
carbon sinks	areas that trap carbon and temporarily remove it from the carbon cycle
climate	weather conditions at a particular place over a long period of time
dissolves	becomes taken up by a liquid, resulting in a clear liquid that is the same throughout
enhanced greenhouse effect	additional warming of the atmosphere caused by gases from human activities
equator	an imaginary circle around Earth that is halfway between the north and south poles
fossil fuels	fuels that are the remains of things that lived millions of years ago; for example, coal is a fossil fuel
global warming	the increase in the temperature of the atmosphere that is predicted to result from the enhanced greenhouse effect
greenhouse effect	the increase in the temperature of the atmosphere due to the presence of greenhouse gases
greenhouse gases	gases that let visible light from the Sun reach the surface of Earth. They also absorb heat energy from Earth.
ice ages	periods when the average temperature of Earth was less than now, causing widespread glaciers and ice sheets
Kyoto Protocol	an agreement signed by many countries that limits the production of gases that help to cause global warming
nutrients	chemicals that a living thing needs to live and grow
photosynthesis	a process in which plants use sunlight and carbon dioxide to make food and oxygen
renewable sources	sources that can replace themselves
subsistence farming	farming that produces enough food for the people on the farm and for future crops
ultraviolet light	light that human eyes cannot detect. It has more energy than visible light.
United Nations	an organization made up of representatives from most countries in the world

Index